John Barry's
Goldfinger
in Focus

by
Barry Russell

Rhinegold Publishing Ltd
241 Shaftesbury Avenue
London WC2H 8TF
Telephone: 020 7333 1720
Fax: 020 7333 1765
www.rhinegold.co.uk

Focus Guides from Rhinegold Publishing
Madonna: *The Immaculate Collection* in Focus
The Who: *Who's Next* in Focus
Danny Elfman: *Batman* in Focus
Baroque Music in Focus
Modernism in Focus
Romanticism in Focus

Rhinegold Study Guides
(series editor: Paul Terry)
A Student's Guide to Music Technology for the Edexcel AS and A2 Specifications
Listening Tests for Students for the Edexcel AS and A2 Specifications

Students' Guides to GCSE, AS and A2 Music for the AQA, Edexcel and OCR Specifications
Listening Tests for GCSE, AS and A2 Music for the AQA, Edexcel and OCR Specifications
A Student's Guide to GCSE Music for the WJEC Specification

The following books are designed to prepare for and support all GCSE and A-level music courses:
Key Stage 3 Elements
Key Stage 3 Listening Tests: Books 1 and 2
Music Literacy Workbook (for GCSE and A-level)
A Student's Guide to Harmony and Counterpoint (for AS and A2 Music)

Rhinegold Education also publishes Classroom Music, Teaching Drama, Rhinegold Dictionary of Music in Sound, Rhinegold Guide to Music Education, and study guides for Classical Civilisation, Drama and Theatre Studies, Performance Studies, Religious Studies.

First published 2007 in Great Britain by Rhinegold Publishing Ltd
241 Shaftesbury Avenue
London WC2H 8TF
Telephone: 020 7333 1720
Fax: 020 7333 1765
www.rhinegold.co.uk

**You should always check the current requirements of the examination, since these may change. Copies of the Edexcel Specification may be obtained from Edexcel Examinations at Edexcel Publications, Adamsway, Mansfield, Nottinghamshire, NG18 4FN
Telephone 01623 467467, Fax 01623 450481, Email publications@linneydirect.com
See also the Edexcel website at www.edexcel.org.uk**

Barry Russell: *Goldfinger* in Focus
British Library Cataloguing in Publication Data.
A catalogue record for this book is available from the British Library.

ISBN: 978-1-906178-10-9

Printed in Great Britain by Thanet Press Ltd

Contents

1   Introduction 5

2   The score 8

3   Analysis of cues in the film 15

        Bond Back In Action Again 15

        Main Title.. 16

        Into Miami 17

        Golden Girl... 18

        Alpine Drive 19

        Auric's Factory... 20

        Death of Tilly 21

        The Laser Beam 22

        Pussy Galore's Flying Circus 22

        Teasing the Korean..................................... 23

        Gassing the Gangsters 23

        Oddjob's Pressing Engagement.......................... 24

        Dawn Raid on Fort Knox................................ 25

        The Arrival of the Bomb and Countdown 28

        The Death of Goldfinger — End Titles................. 29

        Goldfinger — Instrumental 29

4   Context.. 30

5   Appendix 37

The Author

Barry Russell is professor of community music at Leeds College of Music. He has worked as a secondary school teacher, community musician, senior lecturer and artist in residence (pianist/performer/composer) at University College Bretton Hall. He performs with the Cornelius Cardew Ensemble and the Pound Shop Boys, and works throughout Europe as a freelance composer and animateur.

Russell has acted as composer in association for Oldham Metropolitan Borough, education advisor to the Young Musicians Festival, and as an adjudicator for the National Festival of Music for Youth. He has directed education and community projects with several leading orchestras, including the BBC Philharmonic, Northern Sinfonia, City of Birmingham Symphony Orchestra, London Philharmonic Orchestra, Britten Sinfonia, Manchester Camerata, Royal Liverpool Philharmonic Orchestra and NOEL.

Russell is the co-author of *The GCSE Composition Course* (with Tony Harris), published by Peters Edition, and author of *Music and Environment*, a KS2 music-making classroom resource published by BBC Proms in 2002.

Acknowledgements

Barry Russell would like to thank Tony Harris, Julia Winterson and Janet Wilkins for their support and assistance during the preparation of this book.

The author would also like to thank David Ventura for his advice and suggestions. Thanks also to Sarah Smith, Elisabeth Boulton, Ben Robbins, Emma Findlow and Hallam Bannister, of Rhinegold Publishing for their assistance throughout the editing and production process.

Copyright notices

1
Introduction

James Bond from page to screen

James Bond, the hero of a series of novels by Ian Fleming, is quintessentially British, timelessly stylish, a sex god and a lover of gadgets and fast cars. He seeks out and eliminates larger than life villains, wrecking their dastardly plans, pausing only to quaff martinis (shaken – not stirred). The world has grown to love Bond, James Bond.

Unsurprising then that the novels should be turned into a series of movies, each more extravagant and epic, trying to outdo each other with their jaw-dropping special effects and stunts. The success of the Bond movies is built

> In 1952 Ian Flaming wrote *Casino Royale*, the first in a series of twelve novels to feature the fictional secrets agent James Bond 007.

on the simplicity of the premise – good triumphs over evil. Despite the lack of political correctness – cold-blooded killings followed by a throw-away laughter line, a strings of beauties seduced and abandoned – for generations of men their closet desires and wishes are fulfilled onscreen (the 60:40 male to female ratio for audience suggests that they *are* the target audience). It is suggested that more than half the world's population has seen a Bond film. They are repeated year after year on TV and no-one objects. In Britain they are a national institution, the twanging guitar melody instantly recognisable.

With each new film and each new Bond (Sean Connery, George Lazenby, Roger Moore, Timothy Dalton, Pierce Brosnan, Daniel Craig) the brand is reinvented and re-imagined. The *James Bond Theme* is always present, but around it new musical worlds are created, giving each film an identity of its own.

John Barry was the orchestrator of the main *James Bond Theme*, originally composed by Monty Norman, and has written the scores for 11 of the movies. The score for *Goldfinger* is reported to be his favourite, the one which captures the times, places and moods most perfectly. The theme song (with lyrics by Antony Newley and Leslie Bricusse, and given a gloriously over-the-top performance by Shirley Bassey) had success beyond the film and also acted as a marketing tool. More importantly, the song provides thematic material for the rest of the score so that the complete film score is an entity rather than a succession of unrelated numbers and cues.

The soundtrack album sold fairly well in the UK, but in America *Goldfinger* knocked the Beatles' *A Hard Day's Night* from the top of the album charts, winning John Barry his first gold disc. The US album left out the tracks 'Golden Girl', 'Death of Tilley', 'The Laser Beam', and 'Pussy Galore's Flying Circus' which were all contained in the UK release, but included an instrumental version of the main theme. The text below refers to the re-issue of the original soundtrack conducted by John Barry and recorded at CTS Studios, London in July 1964, which includes the US tracks. All the tracks have now been digitally re-mastered.

> Re-mastering is where you take the two-track stereo and apply processing to it. The aim of re-mastering is to make the tracks sound as good as possible and consistent with other commercial releases in the same genre, making them cleaner, clearer, brighter and louder. It is often done when an older analogue recording is re-released in digital format.

Film and character synopsis

In the now trademark action sequence, Bond (Sean Connery) blows up a Mexican drug baron's base (music cue: 'Bond Back in Action Again'). This is followed by the music cue: 'Main Title – Goldfinger'.

The plot begins in Miami Beach (music cue: 'Into Miami') where Bond is investigating the affairs of Auric Goldfinger, a multi-millionaire gold bullion dealer suspected by the Bank of England of stockpiling huge amounts of gold. Bond seduces Goldfinger's assistant Jill Masterson. Later he is knocked unconscious by a sinister bowler-hatted figure. Waking, he finds the body of Masterson in his bed, asphyxiated by a layer of gold paint (music cue: 'Golden Girl') covering her body.

Back in London, Bond makes his traditional visit to Q to collect the latest gadgets – magnetic homing devices and a heavily modified gold Aston Martin DB5, which features machine guns, an oil slick sprayer, a smokescreen generator and a passenger ejector seat.

Bond plays a game of golf with Goldfinger, whose caddie is the bowler-hatted Korean Oddjob. Goldfinger loses and warns Bond not to tangle with him. Oddjob underlines this by decapitating a nearby statue with his steel-rimmed bowler hat.

Bond follows Goldfinger to Switzerland (music cue: 'Alpine Drive'). On the way he meets Tilly Masterson who is out to avenge the death of her sister Jill. He finds the premises of Auric Enterprises (music cue: 'Auric's Factory') and breaks in that night. He finds a team of technicians dismantling Goldfinger's car which is made entirely of gold. Tilly joins him but the guards are alerted to their presence. Tilly is killed by Oddjob (music cue: 'Death of Tilly') and Bond is captured.

During the interrogation, Bond finds himself strapped to a metal table with Goldfinger sending a laser closer and closer towards Bond's groin (music cue: 'The Laser Beam'). Bond talks his way out by mentioning Operation Grand Slam. Realising that Bond is worth more to him alive than dead Goldfinger has him shot with a tranquiliser dart. He awakes on a plane piloted by Pussy Galore. They land in Baltimore (music cue: 'Pussy Galore's Flying Circus').

In Baltimore Goldfinger addresses a meeting of America's Mafia bosses and reveals his plans to attack Fort Knox, home of the US gold reserve, using nerve gas (to be sprayed by Pussy Galore's Flying Circus) to crush resistance and then blow his way into the vaults to steal the gold. Bond has managed to trick his way out of his cell (music cue: 'Teasing the Korean') and has heard the whole plan. Goldfinger kills the gangsters who are no longer of use to him, having delivered the nerve gas (music cue: 'Gassing the Gangsters').

Bond has managed to place a note on Goldfinger's plans, along with a tracking device, in the pocket of a gangster (Solo) who has left early. Solo is shot by Oddjob and the car with the gangster's body still inside is crushed in a scrapyard (Music cue: 'Oddjob's Pressing Engagement'). Bond is recaptured.

Bond tells Goldfinger that Operation Grand Slam can't work. Goldfinger then reveals his true plan – to detonate a Chinese atomic device inside the vault, irradiating the gold and rendering it unusable. As a result, the Chinese hope to cause economic instability for the west and Goldfinger hopes that his stockpile of bullion will increase in value tenfold.

Pussy sends her Flying Circus on their mission to spray the lethal nerve gas over Fort Knox (music cue: 'Dawn Raid on Fort Knox'). Oddjob arrives with the Chinese troops and Bond as an unwilling observer. The troops cut in through the Fort's gates with the laser and reach the vaults. Goldfinger arrives and has Bond escort him to the vaults along with the nuclear bomb (music cue: 'The Arrival of Bomb and Count Down'). Outside the base those supposedly killed prepare their counterattack, Pussy having substituted the nerve gas for a harmless gas.

Bond is handcuffed to the bomb. The army foil Goldfinger's escape but he disguises himself as a soldier, turning on his own men in his desperation to escape. Bond fights with Oddjob, embedding his steel-rimmed bowler hat in a metal gate. As Oddjob goes to retrieve his hat Bond applies a high voltage charge from a severed electrical cable. Bond then races against time to defuse the bomb. A CIA agent arrives and defuses it as the digital timer conveniently reaches the number 007.

Bond believes that Goldfinger has got away. However, en route to meet the president of the United States Bond is held at gunpoint by Goldfinger who has taken the place of the pilot. During a struggle Bond fires the gun at a window and Goldfinger is sucked out of the depressurised cabin to his death (music cue: 'The Death of Goldfinger'); Pussy Galore and Bond crash into the sea. A rescue mission is mounted, but Bond and Ms Galore, who have parachuted to safety, are far too busy to be rescued (music cue: 'End Titles').

2
The score

Instrumentation and orchestration in *Goldfinger*

John Barry's film scores have an immediately identifiable signature sound, characterised by the combination of horns (sometimes with trombones and tuba) and strings. For *Goldfinger* he uses an orchestra of strings, brass, harp and percussion with a small contingent of woodwind.

The basis of the orchestral palette for the *Goldfinger* score is a string orchestra (violins 1 and 2, violas, cellos and double basses). Barry takes a great interest in instrumental colours: for example, he often divides the string parts to make richer chord scorings (this is referred to as *divisi*) and uses pizzicato, tremolando and mutes to extend his sonic possibilities.

To this string section he adds four trumpets, four horns, two tenor trombones, bass trombone and tuba (when used in combination, this will be referred to as the brass). Again a range of playing techniques (such as flutter tonguing – playing a note while trilling the letter 'r' with the tongue) and different kinds of mutes (such as cup and harmon mutes) are used for maximum colour effect.

Woodwind is used sparingly in the *Goldfinger* score with occasional contributions from a solo tenor saxophone (for romantic or urban moments) and flute (plus piccolo) and oboe (plus cor anglais), which are used in solo moments and to double and colour string lines.

Barry uses the harp in a variety of ways, for example with glissandi (rapid upwards or downwards sweeps on the strings), chordal accompaniments and melodic lines. He also shows his interest in instrumental colour in

Horns in this context always refers to french horns in F, not the combination of saxophones, trumpets and trombones used as part of the rhythm section in pop, and referred to as the horn section.

String parts mostly consist of single lines: the indication *divisi* instructs players to divide up and share two or more lines between them. The indication *pizzicato* asks players to pluck (returning to *arco* – bowed), *tremolando* is a very fast 'scrub' bowing movement and mutes (indicated by the term *con sordino*) are fixed to the bridge of the instruments and cut out some of the harmonics, producing a muffled, darker coloured sound.

Mutes are fitted to brass instruments in order to change their colour or timbre. Most used is the *straight mute*, cone-shaped, usually made of metal, with three pieces of cork to hold it in the bell of the instrument. The *cup mute* is conical with a cup-shaped bottom covering the bell of the instrument. Special effects mutes include the *bucket mute* which clips over the bell; the *harmon mute* which can be fully inserted, pulled out or removed entirely for a 'wa-wa' effect made by covering and uncovering the stem opening; the *plunger mute* which is shaped like a plumber's plunger and held over the bell and opened or shut; and for very quiet playing players might use a *whispa* or *practice mute*. To listen to examples: www.philharmonia.co.uk/thesoundexchange/the_orchestra/instruments/.

passages which use the lowest strings of the instrument. For example, at the opening of 'Teasing the Korean', where the harp sounds almost like the Kaya-Guhm, the Korean 12-string zither.

The live feel of the recording adds to the edginess and excitement of the music – especially in the big-band style trumpets which play in their upper register creating some split notes.

The score for *Goldfinger* is given homogeneity by constant reference to Auric Goldfinger's home key of F (major and minor) and strong harmonic relationships between the individual cues. Added jazz harmony and some almost folk-type modal harmony sit side by side. The use of leitmotifs binds the whole score together. These easy-to-spot melodic, harmonic and/or rhythmic ideas are related to specific characters and are varied to suit the mood of the particular scene and situation.

> A leitmotif (literally a 'leading motif') is a recurring musical idea (a melody, chord sequence, rhythm or a combination of these) that is associated with a particular person, place or idea in a piece of music. Leitmotifs are used as structural reference points (like a hook in a pop song) and help unify large-scale pieces. Weber used the idea in his operas but the term is particularly associated with the operas of Richard Wagner.

Interestingly, the producers of *Goldfinger* disliked the title song and wanted to replace it but Barry had already cross-referenced the rest of the film score with ideas taken from the song so it had to remain. The song went on to become a worldwide hit, selling more than a million copies in the USA alone, and earned Shirley Bassey a Gold Disc in May 1965. The soundtrack LP reached number one. In the UK the song reached a relatively disappointing number 21 in the charts. Bassey went on to record two more title songs for Bond films: *Diamonds Are Forever* (1971) and *Moonraker* (1979).

John Barry – some musical influences

Barry's lush, vibrant film scores show the influence of the large, symphonic film scores of the thirties. His father owned a string of cinemas and, as a child, Barry was able to watch films over and over again, absorbing the relationship of music to image and the rich romanticism of the film scores of Erich Korngold (*The Prince and the Pauper*, 1937; *The Sea Hawk*, 1940), Franz Waxman (*Captains Courageous*, 1937; *Dr Jekyll and Mr Hyde*, 1941) and Max Steiner (*King Kong*, 1933; *Gone with the Wind*, 1939).

At the outset of his musical career, Barry worked as an arranger for big bands. The influence of writing for this medium, with its clearly delineated trumpet, saxophone, trombone and rhythm sections, is apparent in his sectional use of the orchestra (for example the string section contrasted with the brass section). Barry went on to form a seven-piece jazz group; jazz chord progressions and melodic inflections are often part of the musical vocabulary in his film scores.

The style of music in the *Goldfinger* score is an eclectic mix of pop, big band jazz and broad symphonic ideas. This symphonic style becomes increasingly evident in later John Barry film scores such as *Out of Africa* (1985) and *Dances with Wolves* (1990).

Some other major film scores

John Barry has written scores for a remarkable variety of film genres: war, action, suspense, drama, historical drama, comedy, romance, Western and science fiction. He has yet to write a horror film score but admits to a desire to write the music for a remake of *Frankenstein*. His scores reveal a huge compositional facility and range. His background in jazz comes to the fore in *The Knack... and How to Get It* (1965) where he captures the period exactly with his writing for Hammond organ, and in *The Cotton Club* (1984) where he complements the action with big band jazz and blues. In *The Day of the Locust* (1974), a tale of Hollywood during the depression of the 1930s, soft shoe shuffle and music hall mix with aleatoric music. To notate this Barry used graphic and time/space notation which requires the performers to make their own decisions about parameters such as pitch and volume. He also used these techniques to create soundscapes for *King Kong* (1976) and *The White Buffalo* (1977). Here new instrumental playing techniques and the use of tone clusters show the influence of Penderecki.

> The symphonic style evident in the Korngold, Waxman and Reiner films mentioned on page 9 was repopularised by John Williams with his scores for the *Star Wars* series, *ET* and the *Indiana Jones* films. Now composers such as Danny Elfman (*Batman*, 1989; *Mission: Impossible*, 1996; and *Spider-Man*, 2002), James Horner (*Titanic*, 1997; *Troy*, 2004; and *Apocalypto*, 2006) and Hans Zimmer (*Gladiator*, 2000; *Pirates of the Caribbean: The Curse of the Black Pearl*, 2003; *The Da Vinci Code*, 2006) revel in the huge range of moods and colours offered to them by the full symphony orchestra.

> Penderecki is a Polish avant-garde composer. His music has huge appeal to film composers because of the vast range of instrumental colours he invents. His cello concerto is heard in the soundtrack to *The Exorcist* (1973) and *The Shining* (1980).

The historical drama *The Lion in Winter* (1968) gained Barry the Academy Award (Oscar) for Best Music, Original Score for a Motion Picture as well as a BAFTA (the Anthony Asquith Award for Film Music) and a Golden Globe Award nomination for Best Original Score. The score is notable for the use of unaccompanied choral music and instrumental passages which suggest the style of the period but are authentic John Barry rather than pastiche. For *Mary, Queen of Scots* (1971) he once more produces period music, and again shows a fondness for vocal music. A Bond-style action movie *The Specialist* (1994) also uses a wordless chorus.

For *Jagged Edge* (1985) Barry uses synthesisers. He also employs a solo flute and solo piano. However, apart from some cluster stabs and sfx (sound effects), he uses the synths in a very orchestral way with low 'string' washes and brass sounds – his favourite colours. In *The Scarlet Letter* (1995) synths are again used, this time to simulate native American Indian instruments. The film also uses existing music, such as Samuel Barber's famous *Adagio for Strings*, as part of the score.

Barry makes much use of melodic hooks in his film scores. The opening descending fourth of *Born Free* (1966) is as instantly memorable as the *Goldfinger* idea. In *Midnight Cowboy* (1969) the solo blues harp (harmonica) immediately speaks of urban isolation – a classic example of his uncanny knack of choosing the best instrumental colour to serve the dramatic intention of the film. In blockbusters like *Out of Africa* (1985) and *Dances with Wolves* (1990) Barry is able to let his imagination flow in lushly romantic, epic symphonic scores.

Leitmotifs for Goldfinger

The first musical idea to represent Goldfinger is a pair of chords: F major moving to Db major (sometimes Dbmaj7). In the analyses that follow this is referred to as 'Gold 1'. The sudden shift from tonic to flattened submediant (chords I and flat VI) is simple yet immediately striking. The note F is common to both chords and so provides a link (a pivot note) between them. Many of Barry's film themes are in the key of F, which he admits to using for its lyrical potential, especially when writing for strings.

Goldfinger's second leitmotif is a three note melodic idea – a rising fifth followed by a falling second ('Gold 2'). This is often heard in combination with Gold 1. Notice that a tritone is created between the G in the melodic idea and the Db in the chord. This disturbing interval returns throughout the score.

> The interval of a tritone is created by adding a sharp (augmented) fourth or flat (diminished) fifth above a note. The augmented fourth can be found by counting up three whole tones from the starting note – hence tritone. The tritone is found between the 4th and 7th scale degrees of a major scale (for example, from F to B in the key of C major). In medieval times the interval was known as 'diabolus in musica' – literally the Devil in music, as its presence creates tension and unease.

It is worth noting that the melodic idea Gold 2 is identical to the opening of Mercer and Mancini's song *Moon River* from the film *Breakfast at Tiffany's*. The harmonic and timbral context of each piece makes them completely different musical gestures; they exist in different sound worlds.

The melodic idea Gold 2 is treated as a call and the response is a searing high brass idea: F–A♮–F. The A♮ clashes against the Ab in the Gold 1 chord, creating a brash and exciting dissonance, heightened by the brass playing it with flutter tonguing. (See examples overleaf.)

Goldfinger leitmotifs one and two

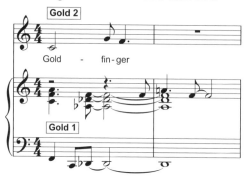

Barry also cleverly uses a melodic fragment from the title song as a leitmotif. He uses the musical phrase with the lyrics 'he's the man' at moments when Goldfinger has succeeded in his dastardly plans. In this context the leitmotif (Gold 3) sounds snide, mocking and smugly triumphant.

Goldfinger leitmotif three

Transformations of the Goldfinger leitmotifs

Barry makes additions to and variations of his leitmotifs to suit the particular dramatic situation. In 'Teasing the Korean' the chordal idea Gold 1 (F to Db) is extended to include a third dark chord – Cmin with an added major 7th over a bass G. This has the effect of adding a more sinister aspect to the leitmotif.

In 'Dawn Raid on Fort Knox' both Gold 1 and Gold 2 undergo many transformations (see analysis, chapter 3 page 25). This is very similar to the ways in which Richard Strauss transforms his character themes in pieces such as *Till Eulenspiegel* and *Don Quixote*.

Leitmotifs for James Bond

Monty Norman composed the original *James Bond Theme* when he was contracted as composer for *Dr No* (1962). The John Barry Seven (Barry's jazz group) were then brought in to add a more contemporary touch to the music. The twangy guitar sound that Barry added makes the theme one of the most instantly

The term *twangy* is not used in a negative sense. This particular guitar sound was popularised by Duane Eddy whose 1959 album is entitled *Twang's the Thang*. The guitar used in the *James Bond Theme* is a Clifford Essex Paragon Cello-Bodied guitar played by Vic Flick.

recognisable in the world. Barry also composed additional music for *Dr No*. In subsequent films the theme and motifs drawn from it are used to herald the presence of the hero.

Bond's first leitmotif (Bond 1) is a pedal note over which the interval of a perfect 5th moves to a minor then major 6th and then falls back down to the minor 6th. This is combined with a crescendo and diminuendo through the two halves of the phrase, which adds to the suspenseful character of the idea.

James Bond's first leitmotif

Bond's second leitmotif (Bond 2) is the famous guitar melody. Some commentators have suggested that the heroic rhythms of the melody are influenced by rhythms from Rossini's *William Tell*. The twanging guitar is very much a sound of its time, found particularly in music for westerns. Listen to the theme tunes for the TV series *The Virginian* (1962) and *Bonanza* (1959), and see how the same sound is used in the middle 8 of title music to the seminal spaghetti western *The Good, The Bad and The Ugly* (1966 music by Ennio Morricone).

James Bond's second leitmotif

Other leitmotifs and key ideas

The timpani are used as a sort of instrumental colour leitmotif throughout the score to add a sense of menace and impending danger (see example overleaf).

Goldfinger

Barry creates a simple 'Menace' leitmotif from three triplet crotchets followed by two straight crotchets. This idea has echoes of the opening rhythm of Beethoven's fifth symphony which has sometimes been called a 'fate motif' but was also used to signify victory in radio broadcasts during World War Two. This idea is heard on timpani and snare drum.

James Bond Menace leitmotif

In the cue 'Auric's Factory' Barry introduces a four note idea, C–B♭–E♭–C to represent Goldfinger's sinister organisation. This is referred to in the analyses as 'Auric 1'.

Auric 1

A three note descending figure, a sort of minor key variation on *Three Blind Mice*, assumes increasing importance in the score, and is associated with failure and defeat.

The cue 'Bond Back In Action Again' opens with dramatic chords which recur throughout the entire score. The chord Em9 (E minor with an added F♯) is always associated with James Bond and will be referred to as the 'Spy' chord.

Throughout the score notice how Barry manipulates the leimotifs in many different ways, for example:

- Accompaniment variations – presenting the leitmotif unchanged but in a new rhythmic or harmonic context
- Playing the leimotif using alternative instrumentation
- Extensions – adding new material to the leitmotif
- Rhythmic transformations – changing the rhythm of melodic and rhythmic leimotifs
- Pitch transformations – keeping the shape of melodic leitmotifs the same while changing the pitches
- Using fragments of the leitmotifs as new ideas which are then subject to the processes of transformation
- Combining associated or contrasting leitmotifs.

3
Analysis of cues from the film

Introduction

The following cues are examined in the order they occur in the film score rather than the track order contained on the CD. This is to help you understand the development of the leitmotifs as the score progresses. As you watch and listen, notice how Barry is happy to let the visuals do the work, often simply underpinning them with static chords and ostinato ideas which heighten the tension. He never resorts to 'Mickey Mousing' – a term derived from cartoon scores where the music exactly matches the action on the screen. Sometimes scenes which would appear to need music (such as the sequence where Bond chases and stops Tilly Masterson's car and similar chase sequences) are left simply with their 'live' sounds.

The relationship of SFX and music in Barry's scores

Goldfinger was made at a time when the trend for film sound effects (sfx) was to exaggerate them. Barry insisted on working with the sound editor to develop ways in which the sound effects became part of the overall soundscape, relating to the music score, blending in and out. This way of working became a Barry trademark. For example, in *Raising the Titanic* (1981) the raising sequence is a symphony of creaks, scrapes and metallic groans, the orchestral music emerging as the ship breaks the surface. In *Dances with Wolves* (1990) the buffalo hunt sequence starts with the thundering sounds of the stampeding creatures and then the music fades in. The natural sounds are complemented by the musical ones.

Bond Back In Action Again

Bar numbers	Music
1–2	The urgent stabbing 'spy' chord opens this cue.
3–4	Bond 1 enters now with...
5–10	...Bond 2 over it, using the unmistakable twangy guitar sound.
11–15	The horns echo the last phrase of the theme without the rhythm section, sounding distant and cautious. Over a held chord Em^6 the music slows (ritardando) into a new tempo.

Goldfinger

Bar numbers	Music
16–19	In this slower tempo the harp plays a three-note idea on the lower strings. This is actually derived from the *James Bond Theme* but now it sounds like Gold 2. Barry moves the placing of this idea across the bar to give the effect of losing the pulse of the music.
20–23	Muted trombones and marimba add a punctuating idea in the original faster tempo.
24–25	The harp returns in the slower tempo.
26–28	A shortened version of the punctuation idea is followed by the strings, using the melodic material from the title song for the words 'He's Mister...' leads back into...
29–32	...Bond 1 high in the strings with pizzicato double basses bringing out the insistent offbeat.
33–36	The *Bond Theme* middle 8 idea is answered by stuttering muted trombones and trumpets.
37–40	Gold 2 is heard in a slightly altered version on saxophone and then horns.
41–50	The marimba enters with a nagging, ticking ostinato played with hard beaters to bring out the high harmonics of the notes.
51–56	The muted brass stuttering idea is played over the top.
57–64	The marimba continues ominously.
65–67	Muted brass play a simple cadential idea – a sort of minor key version of *Three Blind Mice*. This will become important as an idea associated with defeat later in the score.
68–72	A searing high note in the violins brings the cue to a close.

Main Title

This has a classic pop song structure. Much of the credit for the success of this song must go to Shirley Bassey's attention to detail in performance. For example on the words 'spider's touch' she suggests recoiling in disgust in the way she sings the word 'touch' and on the words 'cold finger' the word 'cold' is positively icy. Even colder is her way with 'the kiss of death…'

Section	Music
Introduction – 8 bars	The song opens with the combined leitmotifs Gold 1 and Gold 2 with the high brass response. Here they are transposed into E major (so the Gold 1 becomes E major/C major). This idea is repeated four times with a gradual diminuendo which happens not only by decreasing dynamics but by changing the scoring. Notice the use of acoustic guitar and tambourine in the rhythm section.

Section	Music
Verse – 16 bars	Bassey's vocal line is supported by lush string chords. In the second bar of the verse notice the scurrying five-note unison strings idea, used like a drum fill before they return to rich divisi chords. A solid kick bass drum, pizzicato cellos and basses keep the sense of forward drive. In the repeat of the opening idea, now with the words 'Such a cold finger', horns and trombones are added and the response idea from Goldfinger's leitmotif is heard. The harmony is very adventurous – note the shift from A major to E♭ major in bars 12–13 and from E♭ to B major in bars 14–15. The first shift has the tritone relationship that is such a feature of the score and the second uses an *enharmonic* relationship – the E♭ in the first chord is used as a pivot note, becoming a D♯ in the second chord. Notice also how with the harmony on 'a spider's touch' the music doesn't enter his web of sin, the E♭ major wants to resolve into A♭ minor but pulls back. Then on 'but don't go in' the music does enter the web of sin, modulating into A♭ minor.
Middle 8	Barry introduces the leitmotif Bond 1 into the accompaniment on brass with a hint of the *Bond Theme* middle 8 on violins. The harmony is always shifting restlessly and the music moves straight into E♭ minor on 'Golden words'. Muted trumpets add staccato stabs. Finding himself in G♭ minor at bar 31 (a tone above the home key of E major), Barry uses a diminished 7th chord in bar 32 to return to the opening of the verse.
Verse – 8 bars only	The sequence from bars 17–24 is repeated with new words.
Middle 8	As above.
Verse – 8 bars only	As above.
Outro	Over Bond 1 the warning 'He loves only gold' is repeated more and more urgently by Bassey.

Goldfinger middle 8 and chords

Into Miami

In this glitzy jazz waltz, a mere 34 bars long, Barry immediately establishes a glamorous atmosphere to match the screen images of skyscapers and luxury living.

Goldfinger

Barry's background in jazz comes to the fore but notice also the alternating two-chord patterns of the accompaniment which suggest the influence of Erik Satie's *Gymnopedies*. The solo tenor saxophone is immediately sassy, sexy and urban.

Bar numbers	Music
1–4	Intro – a two-chord pattern is established: A♭m to D♭⁷. A gritty feeling is given by the growling bass trombone and tuba on the bass line, beefed up by a solid kick bass drum. Glissandi from the harp hints at luxury while the whole is bedded on lush divisi string chords.
5–12	The trumpets enter with an angular melody which rises to a perfect 4th and then falls on a tritone – D♭ to G. In the repeat of the four-bar melody the perfect tritone rises to pave the way for the entry of the saxophone.
13–20	A new chord progression is established which again alternates two chords – A♭m and B♭m⁶. This is very similar to the chord sequence of the jazz standard *Summertime* by George Gershwin. The saxophone has new melodic material. This middle 8 is improvisatory in character but related to the four-bar idea heard previously.
21–28	The trumpets repeat their four-bar tutti and the accompaniment returns to the first chord sequence.
29–32	In the outro, divisi strings add the notes B♭ and F to the A♭ minor feel, creating an added sixth and ninth – one of Barry's favourite jazz harmonies.
33–34	The strings resolve onto the tonic major of A♭.

Golden Girl

Notice Barry's use of a simple colouristic device here – the shiny metallic sounds suggest the sheen of gold on the dead girl.

Bar numbers	Music
1–4	Horns, trombones and tuba play Gold 1 in the F–D♭⁷ version to which Barry adds a C minor (major 7th) chord, punched out twice forcefully. Notice the timpani and pizzicato basses hinting at Bond 1 with the offbeat figure. Crotales (tuned metal discs), harp and xylophone (bright sounds suggesting the play of light on gold) enter with a two-note descending figure C–B derived from the new chord sequence.
5–12	Low brass play Gold 1, including the new chord at half the speed of the previous section, suggesting a funeral cortege.
13–14	Crotales, harp and xylophone accompany a new version of Gold 2, on cellos now, with the descending minor 2nd idea added by a flutter-tongued flute.
15–16	The same idea is repeated by harp answered by marimba (rolling the notes).
17–26	The harp introduces a new idea C–G–D–E–A♭ over an F major chord (with its A♭) richly scored for muted trombones, low strings and marimba playing a rolled chord with four mallets. The timpani keep up their funereal beat.

Bar numbers	Music
27–30	Trumpets and trombones enter using Auric 1 and the music slips back into the minor. The horns play a variant of the previous harp figure and this is taken up by the violins against an Fm chord played by trumpets with harmon mutes – producing a bright, metallic sound.
31–32	The cue ends with a low Fm chord on strings and harp.

Alpine Drive

Bar numbers	Music	Time	Action
1–2	Goldfinger's leitmotif F–Db is presented in a new version. The Db chord has an added major 7th enriching it. Unison violins play the Goldfinger theme C–G–F falling onto an E as...	0'00"	An airport official confirms Bond's flight to Geneva.
3–4	Muted trumpets (with harmon mutes making a tight metallic sound) and harp play a stab on C, which is unsettled by the timpani playing a tritone idea on C–F♯.	0'06"	Bond checks that the tracking device he secreted in Goldfinger's car boot is still functioning.
5–10	A lush version of the main title song has a characteristic Barry sound – the violins take the vocal line with the horns, trombones and tuba provide rich backing harmonies.	0'12" – 0'25"	The scene changes to the Swiss Alps. Oddjob is driving Auric Goldfinger, a harp glissando signals our first sight of them. Bond's car is seen following Goldfinger.
11–12	The trombone interpolation C–Db–C–Db–C hints at James Bond's leitmotif Bond 1.	0'30"	Bond checks his tracking device.
13–18	The violins take the melody up an octave with suave harp glissandi, pizzicato cellos and double basses against smooth, sustaining brass.	0'35" – 0'42"	Goldfinger's car climbs higher into the mountains. Cut back to Bond following.
19–24	Bond 1 leitmotif in A minor. The middle 8 vocal line is taken by unison horns. At bar 22 (1'08") Barry introduces a double-time feel with ride cymbal played with brushes and a walking bass. Divisi violins enrich the sound world and smears (short glissandi) between notes add a seedy element.	0'52" – 1'08"	Tilley Masterson's car appears, following Bond. She sounds her horn to get past him. Bond sees that she is an attractive woman. He tries to keep his mind on the job in hand ('Discipline 007').

Bar numbers	Music	Time	Action
25–29	The music returns to the original tempo feel and a flute trill on E provides a transition back to the verse melody.	1'20"	Tilly Masterson drives on. Bond checks the tracking monitor.
30–33	The flow of the music is interrupted by a sudden string tremolando G♯ (played *fp*). This E major chord resolves into A minor with the violins in their highest register. Harp and pizzicato strings hint at Bond 1.	1'32"	Bond sees from the monitor that Goldfinger's car has stopped.
		1'46"	Sequence ends.

Auric's Factory

It is important to note that in the film this cue is played a semitone higher; the analysis that follows is based on the soundtrack CD.

Bar numbers	Music	Time	Action
1–8	Over a low pedal F in the basses the horns introduce a new idea C–B♭–E♭–C (Auric 1), with the cellos adding a glissando smear from the B♭ to the E♭. Notice how Barry pulls the tempo around – lingering over the ends of bars with a pause at the end of bar 8.	0'00" – 0'15"	Bond eventually finds Auric's factory – Auric Enterprises. He looks above the factory to the wooded hills. Cut to Bond hiding in the trees and working out how he will infiltrate the factory. He sees Goldfinger's car.
9–33	A faster tempo is established in D minor with a new time signature $\frac{2}{4}$, and irregular stabbing muted brass dyads (two-note chords) D and F against a high pedal F played tremolando by the violins. In bars 15–16 the timpani play Auric 1 in a new version, DDCDFDA. The stabs continue and the timpani repeat Auric 1.	0'30"	Night has fallen. Bond, all in black, penetrates the factory, avoiding the guards (0'49" and 0'58"). At 1'06" he climbs over a wall marked 'Eintritt Strengstens Verboten' (entry strictly forbidden).
34–55	The lower instruments are added and the note C is introduced as a pedal (D minor/C). The irregular stabs continue.	1'15"	Bond has reached the roof of the factory. He looks in and sees the workers melting down Goldfinger's car – the bodywork of which is made of 18-carat gold.
56–68	The high pedal with stabs reappears.	2'03"	The music changes at the mention of Operation Grand Slam. Bond makes his getaway.

Bar numbers	Music	Time	Action
69–76	The music returns to F minor with a slower tempo in $\frac{4}{4}$. The opulent sound of the harp is reinforced by throbbing vibraphone (played with the motor on to create a wah effect). The harp ostinato is a falling second, G–F, the 'finger' from 'Goldfinger' (Gold 2).	2'20"	Safely back in the woods, Bond finds Tilly Masterson armed with a rifle, looking to avenge the death of her sister.
77–78	The brass enter to reinforce the sound and the cue ends with the familiar stabbing 'Spy' chord.	2'54"	Bond tackles Tilly to the ground and her gun trips an alarm wire – this is synced with the stabbing chord. An alarm sounds.

Death of Tilly

This cue is a variation of the cue 'Golden Girl'. Barry uses this idea to show that Tilly and Jill are sisters.

Bar numbers	Music
1–2	Gold 1 in the original version is followed by C minor. A snare drum is added and now there are three punchy chords. The strings have a two-note anacrusis. This an octave G to G and leads into:
3–5	A held pedal note G below which the harp in its lowest register, and doubled by double basses, plays a simple idea: a C minor triad followed by a G minor triad ending with the notes F–G (notes two and three of Gold 2 reversed). The cellos have an anacrusis into...
6–8	...A new idea beginning with a falling figure with an emphasis on the second note of each group of three: G–E♭–D G–D–C. This sad, lamenting idea is very similar to the slow movement of Shostakovich's fifth symphony. A timpani figure gives us a pick-up into...
9–10	...A forceful chord of C minor in the horns and trombones.
11–14	A steady, relentless harp ostinato AGADCGAE♭A (giving a feel of Cm^{6+9}) accompanies a repeat of the lamenting idea in the cellos. The violins sustain their pedal note G throughout.
15–30	The harp ostinato and violin pedal continue. Muted trumpets and flute have an insistent two-note interruption using the dyad A and C. This is spaced irregularly and suggests the death throes of the victim. Flute and oboe add a plaintive sustained A at bar 29.
31–33	Suddenly the music plunges into C minor. Horns then trumpets play the figure E♭–B♮ over the held chord, creating (major 7th).

The Laser Beam

Like the Dawn Raid sequence, this is an exercise in building and layering ostinato patterns.

Bar numbers	Music
1–8	A two-bar idea is repeated four times. In the first bar strings sustain an F chord with an added second. In the second bar muted trumpets with a harp are answered by a marimba. This uses the so called 'fate' motif from the beginning of Beethoven's fifth symphony.
9–16	Over this ostinato, Gold 2 is played twice by the cellos, tremolando, which then goes on to sustain a G – the added second which creates tension.
17–20	The violins play Gold 2 which is now extended by repeating the two falling notes a note higher, so G–F becomes A♭–G.
21–24	This extended version is repeated an octave higher.
25–28	The extended idea becomes the beginning of a new ostinato figure in the violins. The nagging of these falling seconds is exaggerated at the beginning of the pattern by a glissando – a sickening effect echoing Bond's concerns for his safety.
29–32	A high pedal F is heard and the middle brass enter to thicken the texture.
33–36	Now the low brass enter. Simply by adding instruments and (thickening the texture) getting louder the music becomes almost unbearably tense.
37–44	The violin ostinato is reduced to just the two-note extension idea of Gold 1. The heat is taken out of the music by a coldly scored Fm chord for divisi solo strings.

Pussy Galore's Flying Circus

Bar numbers	Music
1–4	This cue begins with a jolly $\frac{12}{8}$ feel, and a carousel-like riff in violins and flutes with a variation of Gold 2 on horns. The harmony moves from F major to D♭ major 7.
5–8	The jolly mood evaporates with the music taking on sombre colours and side-slipping onto the dark C minor (major 7) chord in bar Cm7.
9–20	The tempo picks up now (poco piu mosso) and the harmony oscillates between F major and C minor (major 7).
21–30	The violins enter, tremolando, with a new variation of Gold 2.
31–32	The crotales, their bright sounds suggesting the play of light on gold (or the lust for gold), enter with a two-note descending figure C–B heard previously in the 'Golden Girl' cue. Repetition of ideas and sequences like this helps bind the score together.
33–36	The trombones play Gold 1 in its plainest version.
37–42	The $\frac{12}{8}$ feel returns with harp glissandi suggesting aerobatic stunts.

Bar numbers	Music
43–46	The brass play Gold 1 and 2 with the saxophone providing a racy, sexually charged commentary.
47–54	The strings play a version of the Goldfinger leitmotif, smearing between notes a 2nd apart in a provocative way. A solo trumpet with wah mute (a harmon mute with the tube removed) adds to the racy tone, reflecting the attractiveness of Pussy Galore's female colleagues.

Teasing the Korean

Bar numbers	Music
1–4	Strings sustain a low Fm chord. The harp on its lowest strings plays the Auric 1 leitmotif followed by the notes A♭ and C which confirm the F minor of Goldfinger. This is followed (bar 3) by a chord combining C, D♭ and G – the tritone is there again.
5–10	The previous music is repeated and extended.
11–13	The saxophone plays a new, jazz-inflected version of Gold 2 combined with Auric 1.
14–18	The strings repeat this idea but end on a high F. Horns, trumpets and then the piccolo (in its shrill highest register) hint at Gold 2 in a new version. The Bond 'spy' chord is combined with the second and third notes of Gold 2.
19–20	The cor anglais plays the solo heard on the saxophone earlier.
21–25	With the strings sustaining a high Fm chord the brass, snare drum and timpani play a forceful version of the Menace idea heard in 'Bond Back in Action'.
25–32	Against a sustained strings chord the harp plays a new version of Gold 2, harmonised with Barry's favourite Fm^6 chord. This is answered with an echo of the Menace idea on timpani with pizzicato cellos and basses.

Gassing the Gangsters

This short cue – just over a minute of music – is a masterclass in instrumental colour and shows Barry fully exploiting the resources of the limited orchestral palette he has chosen.

Bar numbers	Music
1–8	Gold 1 on trombones and horns is played in the expanded version first heard in 'Golden Girl': F major – D♭ major 7 – C minor (major 7) resolving back to F major. The C minor (major 7) chord is sour and unsettling. The chords crescendo and the overall section dynamic increases. Notice the presence of timpani reinforced by pizzicato double basses.
9–10	Trumpets in their low register add to the menacing feel.
11–12	A high, ringing metal crotale plus a high xylophone played with hard sticks reflect Barry's feel for instrumental colour.

Bar numbers	Music
13–19	A new, even more urgent version of the Menace idea is heard followed by a screaming idea on muted trumpet, flute and piccolo.
20–21	The music's resolution comes with Gold 2 over an F major chord but it sounds hollow and callous in the context of what has happened on-screen.

Oddjob's Pressing Engagement

Bar numbers	Music
1–3	Brass and strings enter with a chord of C⁷♭⁵). This gives a disorientating feeling because of the tritone C–G♭. A single note from the harp triggers the entry of the violins playing 'The kiss of death' idea from the title song. This leads into...
4–7	...The Bond 1 leitmotif. Notice the insistent offbeat trombones.
8–11	Over this we hear the middle 8 of the *Bond Theme* played firstly on trombones and then on trumpets.
12–13	A two-bar link using a variation of Auric 1 in the bass (F♯–C–E) with a C⁷ chord over it leads into...
14–17	...Strings playing the Gold 1 leitmotif. An elaborate timpani part (played with hard sticks for emphasis) adds a new threatening edge to the music.
18–23	The melodic leitmotif Gold 2 is heard in trumpets and horns.
24–27	Using the phrase 'He's the man, the man with the Midas touch', the music modulates to...
28–35	...A minor for Bond 1, which is now combined with Gold 2 to show the conflict between the two men.
36–39	The opening C⁷♭⁵ chord returns over a pedal G♭ which accentuates the tritone (C–G♭). A solo harp outlines the chord with the figure C–B♭–E–G♭.
40–44	The lower brass pulse the chord and a flute enters, playing with flutter tonguing. This adds a raw, nervous edginess to the music. (Note: bars 41–43 are in $\frac{3}{4}$).
45–48	Gold 1 returns with the timpani adding an exciting counterpoint.
49–52	Gold 2 on trumpets.
53–56	Again the phrase 'He's the man, the man with the Midas touch' is used to modulate to...
57–66	...A minor for Bond 1 with Gold 2 added at bar 61, and the melodic phrase from the Outro of the title song 'He loves only gold' on trombones and then horns.
67–69	Now, in a slower tempo, the brass flutter tongue the Gold 2 leitmotif making it sound rasping and blatant, as if Goldfinger were challenging and goading Bond.

Bar numbers	Music
70–76	The oboe and saxophone introduce a new idea in F minor which ends with the first two notes of Gold 2 – the music only hints at it. The brass and timpani confirm the Goldfinger connection by underpinning this with a solid, pulsing Fm chord.
77–80	Now the music hints at Bond 1 and like Gold 2 previously it is truncated.
81–82	The Menace leitmotif is played twice before...
83–85	...The oboe and saxophone cheekily wind the cue down into silence.

Dawn Raid on Fort Knox

This relentless music is built through layers of ostinati, which build to climaxes before then starting again. The influence of Ravel's *Bolero* might be suggested but the model of the relentless march from Shostakovich's *Leningrad* Symphony No 7 is clear, especially in the bass figure heard right at the outset. This cue could form the model for a composition in which copy and paste 'units' are combined and layered in different ways. A transcription of the opening of this cue can be found in the *AQA GCSE Anthology of Music* (Edition Peters EP 7657).

Note: the timings refer to the film score not the soundtrack CD. Some sections are shortened in the soundtrack CD for musical reasons.

Bar numbers	Music	Time	Action
1–4	Over a new version of the F/D♭ Goldfinger chord leitmotif, Gold 1, the snare drum establishes a militaristic feel with a driving rhythm.	0'00"	Pussy Galore's Flying Circus taxi in preparation for their nerve gas attack on Fort Knox.
5–8	The violins, with oboe and flute, play a long held C on which they crescendo and diminuendo. This is the first note of Gold 2 – simply 'Gold'.		
9–12	Trumpets play Gold 2 in a new version ending C–E–G with the G held to produce a major 9th with the F chord and an augmented 4th added to the D♭ chord.		
13–14	The violins introduce a running semiquaver idea which continues as a layer beneath...	0'24"	The plane takes off.
15–25	...The trumpets repeat Gold 2 and now the piccolo adds the new ending with an answering call from the trumpets which then repeat bars 9 to 12.		

Goldfinger

Bar numbers	Music	Time	Action
26–29	The music is halted in its tracks by a sudden, unexpected D♭7 chord with the tritone G–D♭ forcefully declaimed by timpani, trombones and tuba while the snare drum pounds out the Menace leitmotif.	0'50"	The squadron leader orders 'Commence dive – now'.
30–31	The trumpets scream out a raucous, high F chord answered by horns and trombones with a D♭ chord over a new bass ostinato F–C–D♭–A♭.	0'55"	Fort Knox is sighted in the distance.
32–33	The violins return with their running semiquavers.		
34–37	The Menace music from bars 26 to 29 returns.		Squadron leader orders 'Commence spray on countdown'.
38–41	The raucous high trumpets return.	1'10"	The planes begin to spray their cargo of gas over and around Fort Knox.
42–45	The extended version of Gold 2 returns in a new, high-pitched orchestration with the piccolo doubling the violins to cut through the texture.		
46–49	The new ending of Gold 2 is transformed into a staccato xylophone idea suggesting rapid gunfire.		
50–53	The horns play Gold 2 in its new guise.		
54–57	The staccato xylophone returns.		
58–59	The violins return with their running semiquavers.	1'50"	Platoon after platoon of soldiers are knocked out by the gas.
60–63	The violins and piccolo play a falling minor 2nd idea, E–E♭. This is similar to the extension to Gold 2 but also suggests Bond 3 taken from the end of the first phrase of his theme. However the idea is answered by the horns which play a variation on Gold 2: C–E–E♭.		
64–67	The staccato xylophone returns but now the E♮ has turned to an E♭.		

Bar numbers	Music	Time	Action
68–78	Violins and piccolo play the falling E–E♭ idea answered by horns. Timpani pound triumphantly throughout.		
79–80	Two bars of the Menace idea from bar 26 lead into...		
81–84	...A darkly scored chord of Cm with triumphant percussion.	2'30"	Scenes of devastation. Hundreds of soldiers lie unconscious, knocked out by the gas dropped by Pussy Galore's Flying Circus.
85–93	Over the Cm chord the note D (the added 9th) is heard ever higher, played by oboe, then flute and piccolo, and eventually violins playing a high harmonic.		
94–101	A new version of the Menace section shows us that the operation is going as planned.		
102–109	Over the obsessive snare drum rhythm, the strings play a nervous, intermittent Cmin^9 (the 'Spy' chord). N.B. to match the on-screen action this section is considerably extended.	3'13"	Goldfinger's forces move in towards Fort Knox. As they drive they pass more soldiers knocked out by the nerve gas.
110–113	A further stripped-down version of the Menace section is heard over a timpani roll pedal.	3'55"	The convoy reaches the drive leading up to Fort Knox.
114–121	Percussion and strings play their nervous idea. N.B. to match the on-screen action this section is considerably extended.	4'03"	We see that the two American agents looking after Bond have also been knocked out. The convoy drives up to the gates and, after checking that the nerve gas has dispersed, they set a massive explosive device against the gates.
122–125	The Menace section recurs in its original form.	5'07"	The gates are blown and Goldfinger's forces enter the grounds of Fort Knox.
126–129	The raucous high trumpets return.		
130–133	The extended version of Gold 2 returns in its high-pitched (piccolo and high violins) orchestration.		
134–137	The xylophone motif returns.		

Bar numbers	Music	Time	Action
138–139	The Menace motif subsides into...	5'43"	The laser beam is set up. Notice how its electronic thrum (synthesiser) is a triplet figure against the pulse of the soundtrack.
140–153	...The darkly scored Cm 'Spy' chord – adding the 9th (D) as before.		
154–169	The xylophone enters with the major 7th (B♮), reintroducing the third chord of Goldfinger's leitmotif Gold 1. This is supported by a sustained violin note. The timpani and lower strings hammer out a single note idea, sometimes on the beat, sometimes syncopated, adding tension to the music.	6'12"	The laser beam is aimed at the doors of Fort Knox and begins to cut through.
170–173	The music resolves onto a held C on low trumpets and timpani.	6'46"	The gate falls and is dragged away.

The Arrival of the Bomb and Countdown

In this cue, ideas from the 'Dawn Raid' sequence are fragmented (broken up into smaller musical units).

Bar numbers	Music
1–8	We are now in a much slower tempo than the 'Dawn Raid' section, but this makes the atmosphere even more tense. Repeated Cm chords scored for low strings and heavily accented show the gravity of the situation. Martial timpani and fragments of the snare drum idea from the 'Dawn Raid' punctuate the music.
9–12	Muted low trumpets play Gold 3 ('He's the man') over the strings adding the falling minor 2nd idea first heard in the Golden Girl cue.
13–16	This music is repeated, now on high violins and flute.
17–26	The xylophone (doubled by violins) plays a fragment of its B♮ idea from 'Dawn Raid', now broken and shortened and answered by the oboe (G–B♮).
27–34	After a brief pause, the music changes from $\frac{4}{4}$ to a confident $\frac{6}{8}$. We are back in F minor – Auric's home key with four bars of F minor with added major 7th and 9th; and 4 bars of F minor with a diminished 5th – the tritone returns!
35–42	The falling 2nd idea is transposed into various guises and passed around the strings.
43–50	The Menace motif is heard in a new variation – a hemiola $\frac{3}{4}$ rhythm, pulling against the prevailing $\frac{6}{8}$. Notice the tritone G–D♭ in the trumpets. The stuttering xylophone is heard again, now with glockenspiel added for extra sparkle.
51–58	The lumbering march returns with the falling 2nd idea on strings.

Bar numbers	Music
59–66	The falling 2nd idea moves onto brass and horns.
67–74	The hemiola version of the Menace motif recurs. The xylophone plays a repeated G (part of the tritone idea G–Db) which acts as pivot note as the music...
75–79	...Resolves into C minor, still with the xylophone clattering away.
80–82	Trombones and horns enter with a variation of Gold 2 – opening with the rising 5th before going on to a 'blue' note elaboration.
83–86	The violins play the falling second idea answered by a chilling upward glissando on harp.
87–94	The new Gold 2 variation returns on brass, again answered by violins and harp.
95–102	The music settles on C minor (with a major 7th). The high glockenspiel adds its cynical sparkle to the mix.
103–109	Horns and trumpet introduce a Db (C minor with a minor 9th) which rises to a G – the sinister tritone idea. The bomb is in place.

The Death of Goldfinger — End Titles

Bar numbers	Music
1–4	Barry contrasts sections of the orchestra. The high strings, flute and trumpets play a Ddim7 chord which resolves onto Cm in a totally new orchestral colour with horns, trombones, snare drum and timpani.
5–8	This is repeated and a variation of the Auric 1 leitmotif is heard on horns, trombones and tuba. The snare drum has an extended version of the Danger motif.
9–12	A high string figure in triplets (D–Eb–D) adds to the urgency of the music. Timpani and snare drum play a variation of the Menace leitmotif.
13–18	The horns and then the trumpets play Gold 2, the trumpets ending in their 'screaming' range.
19–27	Against sweeping harp glissandi, the Menace motif is now heard in its original rhythmic form. Here is Barry at his most symphonic and dramatic.
28–30	To counterpoint Goldfinger's death, Barry provides an affecting version of Gold 2, ending with the violins playing a stratospheric version of the melody used for the words 'only gold' – a fitting epitaph.
	The end titles feature a lushly reorchestrated version of the opening song with the horns taking the vocal line.

Goldfinger — Instrumental

This is not included in the film but notice how cleverly Barry re-imagines the song. He is not content just to have the voice replaced by instruments. Throughout Barry uses ideas from the 'Dawn Raid' sequence and the melody is given to twanging guitar as if James Bond himself is singing it.

4
Context

Spy films

The spy fiction genre of novels has always been immensely popular and, unsurprisingly, many have been adapted into films. The spy film genre, a sub genre of action movies, deals with stories of real or fictional espionage.

Alfred Hitchcock made a significant contribution to the genre with *The Man Who Knew Too Much* (1934), *The 39 Steps* (1935), *Sabotage* (1937) and *The Lady Vanishes* (1938). The music for these is symphonic in scope (*The Man Who Knew Too Much*, for example, reaches its denouement in a concert at the Royal Albert Hall). Underscore (evocative and dramatic music) is frenquently counterpointed with diegetic music (music which is part of the on-screen action, for example the Music Hall Band in *The 39 Steps*). The complex interrelationship of music and visuals in Hitchcock's films set the standard for all subsequent screen composers.

Stories of real-life British secret agents were dramatised in the 1940s and early 1950s with films such as *Odette* and *Carve Her Name With Pride* recounting the exploits of Allied agents in occupied Europe. In the 1960s cold war fears and suspicions led to new developments in the spy novel and spy film genres. The realistic spy novels of Len Deighton and John Le Carre were adapted including *The Spy Who Came In from the Cold* (1965) and *Funeral in Berlin* (1967). Their moody, jazz-inflected scores perfectly capture the atmosphere of the era.

John Barry's Bond scores

The character of James Bond was created in Ian Fleming's 1953 novel *Casino Royale*. The novels were adapted for film by producers Harry Saltzman and Albert R Broccoli. The first Bond film, *Dr No,* with Sean Connery as the first in a series of 'Bonds', was released in 1962. Barry wrote the main titles for *Dr No* before going on to write scores for 11 more Bond films starting with *From Russia with Love* (1963). For this he composed an alternative James Bond signature theme *007*, which is featured in four other Bond films (*Thunderball, You Only Live Twice, Diamonds Are Forever, Moonraker*). *Goldfinger*

The John Barry Bond scores include: *Dr No* (1962), for this John Barry elaborated on the *James Bond Theme* on the title credit sequence; *From Russia with Love* (1963), for this he received a Golden Globe Award nomination for Best Song in a Motion Picture; *Goldfinger* (1964); *Thunderball* (1965); *You Only Live Twice* (1967); *On Her Majesty's Secret Service* (1969); *Diamonds Are Forever* (1971); *The Man with the Golden Gun* (1974); *Moonraker* (1979); *Octopussy* (1983); *A View to a Kill* (1985), which gained a Golden Globe Award nomination for Best Original Score for a Motion Picture and for Best Original Song in a Motion Picture); and *The Living Daylights* (1987).

(1964), with its extensive use of leitmotif, is of seminal importance in John Barry's Bond scores.

From Russia With Love (1963) is Barry's first full score for the Bond series. In it he uses many techniques which feature in *Goldfinger*. The title song (actually an instrumental) is in F minor – a favourite key – and a Hammond organ adds a real period touch. Although there are transformations of the melodic material, the technique is not as fully formed as the leitmotif work in *Goldfinger*. Barry is content to let large stretches happen with the 'live' soundscape. The *Bond Theme* (Bond 1 and 2) is used liberally, for example when Bond checks into his hotel in Istanbul and looks for bugging devices. Here the use of the *Bond Theme* tells us Bond is there but doesn't really enhance the tension and mood of the scene. Barry writes some folk music for the belly dance scene in the peasant camp (utilising a klezmer-style clarinet). Elsewhere he uses an eight-quaver beat subdivided into 3+3+2 quavers to give the music an Eastern European flavour (the same rhythm used by Bartók in the last of the *Six Dances in Bulgarian Rhythm* from Book Six of his *Mikrokosmos* collection of piano pieces). Other Barry fingerprints are also present: the use of timpani for moments of foreboding, layered ostinati and brass stabs.

The year after *Goldfinger*, Barry composed the score for *Thunderball*. This is a radically different score, while still containing some of Barry's hallmark ideas. The score is incredibly rich with a much higher proportion of underscore to set moods and heighten tension. Some beautiful timbral effects are realised, for example low flute doubling muted trumpet and, in the underwater battle episode, alto flute and vibes with the motor on slow. A synthesised harpsichord sound is also used. Perhaps the most telling marriage of music and action is the carnival scene. Here diegetic music blends seamlessly into underscore and background.

The scene starts with teams of drummers and revellers in carnival costume as a backdrop to the main action. As the action becomes more intense the underscore kicks in with a snare drum, followed by the orchestra; the innocent carnival music is transformed into something far more sinister by the addition of this layer. The music then melds into a dance-floor scene with the sound of drums (now congas) as a linking sound. The cha-cha turns into a bossanova. The conga player plays wilder and wilder patterns as the tension builds and at the height of his cadenza a shot rings out, the report covered by the drums. The diegetic music reverts to its former, calm cha-cha. This same idea is used in Hitchcock's film *The Man Who Knew Too Much* (1934, remade by Hitchcock in 1956) when the murderer strikes at the loud climax of a concert in the Albert Hall.

In his next score there is again significant use of underscore, but *You Only Live Twice* (1967) also marks a new departure in Barry's writing with many passages of chromatic melody and harmony. This is noticeable in the opening riff of the title song (a riff which Robbie Williams uses in his song *Millennium*). This sinuous melodic idea, heard first on high violins, reappears throughout the score. The scenes in space are accompanied by shifting chromatic harmonies and so we lose our point of (tonal) reference as if floating in space ourselves. In the scene where

Bond's 'body' is recovered, the underwater music recalls the underwater sequence in *Thunderball* with low flute and vibes. Barry's feel for instrumental colour is to the fore: for example, as Bond approaches the sumo match sonorous brass chords (a Barry trademark) are contrasted with a dry guitar ostinato, and in the confrontation at the docks where brass stabs (another trademark) are contrasted with flutter-tongued flute.

Barry imparts Eastern colour by the use of traditional Japanese instruments (samisen and koto) alongside his standard orchestra of strings and brass. He also uses ideas in parallel 5ths to give an oriental flavour to scenes. There are two epic scenes: a battle between Bond in a gyrocopter and the baddies in helicopters; and a scene where, after a rocket is launched, ninja troops storm the volcano headquarters of Blofeld. Both sequences use the layered ostinato technique seen in the 'Dawn Raid' sequence of *Goldfinger*.

In *Diamonds are Forever* (1971), Sean Connery's last outing in the role, we still find the trademark Barry orchestra of strings and brass with solo woodwind and percussion for added colour. There's also some use of synthesisers in one sequence, but submerged in the string textures. Many features of the *Goldfinger* score are also present: high strings doubled with piccolo, brass stabs, chattering xylophone (almost identical to the 'Dawn Raid' sequence), drones, pedals and layered ostinati. Again F is the predominant key and the theme song (in C minor) provides melodic material (C–G–Ab–G–C) which is simply transformed throughout. There is much less use of underscore and there are long stretches with only ambient sound (for example the chase sequences). The Las Vegas sequences are accompanied by louche, jazz-inflected lines which seem to lack the inspiration of the 'Into Miami' cue. As Bond fears immolation, trapped in a coffin in a crematorium furnace, Barry provides some thrillingly over the top symphonic music with a wordless chorus over the orchestra. The attack on Blofeld's oil rig headquarters, a sequence comparable to the 'Dawn Raid', is carried out without music until the closing moments.

Bond title songs

An important aspect of the music for the Bond films has been the title sequence song. These are released in advance of the film as part of the overall marketing strategy. This trend was started in 1952 with the title song of the western *High Noon* 'Do not forsake me oh my darling', sung by Tex Ritter. Other titles songs of the period which acted as pre-publishing for films include *Three Coins in the Fountain* (1954), *Love is a Many-Splendoured Thing* (1955) and *Around the World in Eighty Days* (1956).

The John Barry Bond songs and their singers include: *From Russia with Love* (Matt Monro); *Goldfinger* (Shirley Bassey); *Thunderball* (Tom Jones); *You Only Live Twice* (Nancy Sinatra); *On Her Majesty's Secret Service* (the main theme is performed by the John Barry Orchestra but the film also featured the song *We Have All The Time In The World* performed by Louis Armstrong); *Diamonds Are Forever* (Shirley Bassey); *The Man with the Golden Gun* (Lulu); *Moonraker* (Shirley Bassey); *All Time High* for *Octopussy* (Rita Coolidge); *A View to a Kill* (Duran Duran); and *The Living Daylights* (a-ha).

Music for other spy films

The music for the Jason Bourne series, *The Bourne Identity*, *The Bourne Supremacy*, and *The Bourne Ultimatum* (2002–2007) by John Powell, mixes symphony orchestra and electronic, often metallic sounds on synthesisers. *Mission: Impossible* (1996), starring Tom Cruise and with music by Danny Elfman, uses a large orchestra with digital percussion. *Mission: Impossible II* (2000) with music by Hans Zimmer, also features rock music tracks including *I Disappear* by Metallica, *Take a Look Around* by Limp Bizkit and *Scum of the Earth* by Rob Zombie. Michael Giacchino, the composer of the soundtrack for *Mission: Impossible III,* started out as a composer for video games and so provides a hugely dramatic soundscape for the film. The *Austin Powers* series (1997–2002) often parodies the Bond films and George S Clinton's scores delight in 1970s kitsch pastiche. *Stormbreaker* (2006) features music by Alan Parker, a former member of the bands Blue Mink and The Congregation. Parker worked as an orchestrator for the composer Jerry Goldsmith and is now a successful composer for film and TV, his works including the theme tune to ITN's *News At Ten* and *Coast* for the BBC.

Spy TV shows

The enthusiasm for the spy genre pre-Bond was generated by TV series such as *The Avengers* (1961–1969) and *Danger Man* (1960–1962). Laurie Holloway's music for the former features a jazz big band alongside a string section – a sound world close to John Barry's. For the cult series *The Prisoner* (1964–1966) Ron Grainer composed the *Prisoner* theme. From the 1950s onwards, Grainer worked with the BBC Radiophonic Workshop on a number of television series themes, most famously *Doctor Who* (1963), best known in a electronic realisation by Delia Derbyshire. In complete contrast, he also wrote the theme tunes for *Steptoe and Son* and Rold Dahl's *Tales of the Unexpected*. More recently Jennie Muskett, composer behind the music for the BBC dramas *Spooks* and *The State Within*, combined sampled loops with synthesised material.

Budgets

A film budget is divided into four sections:

- *Above-the-line*: the creative team – writers, composers, art directors
- *Below-the-line*: the overall production costs – the actual shooting of the film
- *Post-production*: the film and soundtrack editing, visual and sound effects
- *Other*: such as insurance, or a completion bond to make sure a film finishes on schedule.

Today the music budget of a major film can be as much as 8%–10% of the total budget. For example, the music budget for *Spider-Man* (2002) was $4.5m (£2.2m) from an overall budget of $139m (£69m). A top film composer (such as

John Williams, Danny Elfman, James Horner) can command a salary in the millions for a film score. An original song or the appearance of a pop star on the soundtrack (such as Christina Aguilera in *Shark Tale*) might add $1m (£500,000) to the bill. Film producers also have to pay for the right to use an existing song (the rights to use Led Zeppelin's *Whole Lotta Love* in the film *Lords of Dogtown* cost producers an incredible $3 million – £1.5m).

As well as paying themselves handsomely, film producers also have to budget for story rights (remaking a film or basing it on a play, novel, or video game), the screenplay, a director, cast (who sometimes receive a share of the film's box-office takings), production costs and visual effects.

Product placement

In Ian Fleming's original novels, James Bond smokes Dunhill cigarettes, drinks Martinis made with Beefeater Gin and wears a Rolex Oyster Perpetual Chronometer. Fleming claimed that by featuring these very real products from the everyday (albeit upper-middle-class) world he was giving Bond an air of reality. In the same way, the films have increasingly featured brands and products to which the audience can aspire. This trend is known as product placement. At the outset placement was subtle so as not to divert attention from the action of the film. These days it is much more overt.

Product placement became big news in the 1970s when tobacco companies recognised the advantages of this approach to brand promotion. Marketing agencies were set up to negotiate deals between product suppliers and film and television producers. To begin with, companies would supply free goods in exchange for placement but now it has become a highly competitive, multi-million dollar industry. Product placement is extremely important in funding a movie. Bond movies are especially popular with advertisers because they appeal to such a wide consumer market.

In some of the Bond films product placement runs out of hand, in fact *Die Another Day* was nicknamed 'Buy Another Day' because of the amount of named brands featured in-shot in the film. These included Samsonite luggage, Omega watches, Bollinger champagne, Heineken beer, a whole range of Sony products and British Airways. Ford motors reportedly paid $35 million (£17.2 million) for the privilege of Bond trading in his famous BMW for an Aston Martin *Vanquish*.

In Casino Royale, the 21st in the Bond movie series, six famous brands enjoy prominent placement – Heineken lager, Ford cars, Smirnoff Vodka, Sony Electronics, Sony Ericsson and Omega watches. These firms between them are rumoured to have spent more than $100 million (£49.2 million pounds – the largest product-placement deal in history at that time) on media and other promotional support for the film. Sony Ericsson phones are referred to by name, and there is a cameo appearance by Richard Branson and Virgin Airlines in Miami Airport. In one scene the love interest Vesper Lynd looks at Bond's wrist and says: 'Beautiful watch. Rolex?'.'No,' replies Bond. 'Omega.'

Product placement can take many forms, the most usual of which are where:

- The product is featured prominently in-shot
- The film's dialogue refers to available products
- Actors in the film use branded products as part of the action.

Product placement in the film *Goldfinger* includes a Rolex watch, the Aston Martin DB5, Dom Perignon champagne and the Lockheed Jet Star. This is almost insignificant compared to Fleming's original novel which mentions in one sequence alone a Chemex coffee machine, a Hoffritz safety razor, Pinaud Elixir shampoo, Phensic painkillers, Sea Island cotton underpants, a Minton egg-cup, groceries from Fortnum and Mason's, and coffee blended by De Bry of New Oxford Street.

The Bond brand is perhaps the most successful franchise in film history. An earlier version of *Casino Royale* (1967) featured music by Burt Bacharach and *Never Say Never Again* (1983) used a score by Michael Legrand but as neither were sanctioned by the franchise, they were denied the right to use the *James Bond Theme*.

Live and Let Die (1973) has a score by The Beatles producer George Martin which lacks symphonic scope and is perhaps more suited to a TV action series. *The Man With The Golden Gun* (1974) drops the guitar version of the *Bond Theme* and goes on to be Barry's least successful Bond score. In his score for *The Spy Who Loved Me* (1977) Marvin Hamlisch dares to update the *James Bond Theme* with a wah-wah guitar. The symphonic style returns in *Moonraker* (1979). The space scenes here use slow-paced, chromatic music similar to the underwater scenes in *Thunderball*. Bill Conti, composer of the 1981 score *For Your Eyes* Only had written the score for *Rocky* (1976), and much of the music betrays this fact. In *Octopussy* (1983) we again find John Barry using timpani to create moments of menace. The title song of *A View to a Kill* (1985), sung by Duran Duran, reached number one in the U.S. music charts and also featured a new Bond theme. The score for *The Living Daylights* (1987) features energetic electronic percussion alongside John Barry's signature orchestral sound.

One of the more critically acclaimed Bond scores not composed by Barry is Michael Kamen's for *Licence to Kill* (1989). Kamen had already produced action film scores such as *Lethal Weapon* (1987) and *Die Hard* (1988), which made him an obvious choice of composer. The title song for *Golden Eye* (1995) was written by U2's Bono and The Edge; Eric Serra was commissioned to write an up to date score including extensive use of samplers and synths. After a poor critical response to the score of the previous Bond film, David Arnold was commissioned to write a conventional Barry-esque score for *Tomorrow Never Dies* (1997) which also features a club-mix of the Bond theme by Moby.

David Arnold went on to write the scores for the next three movies in the series: *The World is Not Enough* (1999), *Die Another Day* (2002) and *Casino Royale* (2006). All of these inhabit the lush symphonic world established by John Barry. After some notable achievements mixed with some miscalculations by a series of composers, Barry's true successor has been found in Arnold. Here is a composer who truly understands Bond's world, and whose music is tailored to the Bond brand. The twenty-second Bond movie is currently in production and the astonishing success of the Bond phenomenon shows no sign of abating, a success due in large part to the symbiotic relationship of music and image within the films.

5
Appendix

Glossary

A capella. Literally means 'in the style of the chapel' (Italian) and refers to vocal music without instrumental accompaniment.

Aleatoric music. Also known as 'chance music'. This is music in which some element of the composition is left to chance, for example by the composer providing several different options for the player(s). The Latin word 'alea' means dice.

Anacrusis. This refers to weak-beat notes which lead in to the first strong beat of a phrase. This is often called a 'pick-up' in jazz and pop music.

Arco. An instruction to a string player to use their bow to play.

Bridge. A short passage that links two different sections often found between a verse and chorus. Sometimes the middle 8 of a song is referred to as the bridge. Musicians may call any different section which appears once within an otherwise repeating form the bridge or middle 8.

Chorus. A setting of the refrain lyrics, it often contains the title words of the song and returns several times. It is normally the catchiest part of the song.

Cluster. A group of notes or pitches immediately adjacent to each other and sounded together.

Coda. The final section of a song. Sometimes referred to as the outro.

Diegetic. Diegetic music is featured music, that is, music played live on-screen as part of the action.

Dissonance. A term applied to harmonies and intervals which create tension in music. The opposite term is consonance.

Divisi. An indication which instructs players to divide up and share two or more lines between them.

Drone. One or more notes (often a perfect 5th) sustained through a passage of music similar to the drone of a bagpipe. Often the musical lines over the drone create dissonances.

Enharmonic. Notes that have an enharmonic relationship sound the same but are written differently because of the harmony to which they relate. For example, C♯ and D♭ might be used in the chord sequence A major to D♭ major.

Fill. A short decorative passage that fills a gap between contrasting patterns.

Flutter tonguing. On woodwind and brass instruments, playing a note while making a 'trrr' sound with the tongue against the teeth.

Genre. A category or type of film, literature or music.

Glissando. The effect of sliding between notes.

Graphic score. A method of musical notation which uses symbols and pictograms to represent sound events.

Hemiola. A rhythmic effect achieved by stressing the first of each pair of notes in a triple-time pattern instead of the first of each three (1–2, 1–2, 1–2 rather than 1–2–3, 1–2–3). The effect is famously used by Bernstein in 'America' from *West Side Story*.

Hook. A catchy musical idea which is memorable and therefore locks itself into the listener's consciousness.

Interval. The difference in pitch between any two notes.

Leitmotif. Literally a 'leading motif'. It is a recurring musical idea (a melody, chord sequence, rhythm or a combination of these) which is associated with a particular person, place or idea in a piece of music.

Mickey Mousing. A term derived from cartoon scores where the music exactly matches the action on the screen.

Middle 8. A contrasting section in a song.

Mutes. These are fixed to the bridge of string instruments and the bells of brass instruments in order to change the timbre.

Ostinato. A rhythmic or melodic pattern which is repeated for a significant amount of time. In pop and jazz this is often referred to as a riff.

Pedal. A single held or repeated note against which changing chords are played.

Pizzicato (pizz.). An indication for players to pluck the strings with their fingers.

Riff. See ostinato.

Sequence. The immediate repetition of a short musical phrase at a different pitch.

SFX. An abbreviation of 'sound effects'.

Soundscape. A piece of music which conjures up an image in the mind.

Stab. A loud, accented single note or chord.

Syncopation. When off-beat notes are accented.

Texture. The melodic, harmonic and instrumental layers of sound; how they combine and interact.

Timbre. Instrumental colour, the quality that makes one sound different from another; for example an electric guitar sounds different from an acoustic guitar.

Time/space notation. A way of notating music so that the distance between notes on a stave suggests their relative durations. The player must decide how the notes relate to each other, for example, notes close together might be played quickly and widely spaced notes might be played as long, slow notes.

Tonic. The first note of a key. Also, the name of a chord built on the first degree of the scale.

Tremolando. An indication to a string player to use very fast 'scrubbing' bow movement.

Triad. A three-note chord, most often used to refer to a chord made up of the root, third and fifth of a scale, but which can describe any three-note chord. A two-note chord is referred to as a *dyad*.

Tritone. The interval between two pitches created by adding a sharp (augmented) fourth or flat (diminished) fifth above or below a note. The augmented fourth can be found by counting up (or down) three whole tones from the starting note – hence the name tritone. The tritone is found between the 4th and 7th scale degrees of a major scale (for example, from F to B in the key of C major).

Tutti. An indication that all members of an ensemble or section are to play together.

Underscore music. This is used to underpin on-screen action, to add atmosphere and tension.

Verse. A section which is repeated each time with different words set to the same melody. Along with the chorus (with which it alternates) this is one of the most important 'building blocks' of a song.